George T Ulmer

Adventures and Reminiscences of a Volunteer

George T Ulmer

Adventures and Reminiscences of a Volunteer

ISBN/EAN: 9783744662932

Printed in Europe, USA, Canada, Australia, Japan

Cover: Foto ©ninafisch / pixelio.de

More available books at **www.hansebooks.com**

OF A

VOLUNTEER,

OR A

Drummer Boy from Maine

BY

GEO. T. ULMER,

COMPANY H, 8TH MAINE VOLUNTEERS.

Dedicated to the Grand Army Republic.

PREFACE.

In submitting this little book the author does not attempt to edit a history of the rebellion, nor does he assume to be correct in the date of events to a day. He does not hope or expect to make a hero of himself by writing it, for he was far from doing anything heroic, believing, as he does, that most of the heroes of the war were killed. Perhaps the WRITING of this book may stamp him a hero, and for his audacity in so doing some one may kill him. But he intends to clothe his little work in homely, rugged, commonplace language. Not striving to make it a work of literary merit, only a truthful account of an unimportant career and experience in the army. It may, perhaps, be interesting to some of his comrades, who recollect the incidents or recall similar events that happened to themselves, and thereby serve the purpose of introducing one of the youngest soldiers and a comrade of that greatest and most noble of all organizations, the Grand Army of the Republic.

Respectfully,

GEORGE T. ULMER.

OMBARDMENT of Fort Sumter. This was the beginning and the first sound of actual war which inspired me, and kindled the fire of patriotism in my youthful breast. The little spark lay smoldering for two long years, 'till at last it burst forth into a full blaze. When Fort Sumter was bombarded, I was a midget of a boy ; a barefooted, ragged newsboy in the city of New York. The bombardment was threatened for several weeks before it actually occurred; and many nights I would have been bankrupted, but that everyone was on the "qui vive" for the event, and I got myself into lots of trouble by shouting occasionally, " Fort Sumter Bombarded !" I needed money ; it sold my papers, and I forgave myself. When the authentic news did come, I think it stirred up within me as big a piece of fighting desire as it did in larger and older people. I mourned the fact that I was then too small to fight, but lived in hopes that the war would last until I should grow. If I could have gone south, I felt that I could have conquered the rebellious faction alone, so confident was I of my fighting abilities.

In the fall of '61 my dear mother died, and my father who had a great desire to make possibilities out of improbabilities, and believing a farm the proper place to bring up a family of boys, bought one away in the interior of Maine. The farm was very hilly, covered with huge pines and liberally planted with granite ledges. I used to think God wanted to be generous to this state and gave it so much land it had to be stood up edgeways. Picture to yourself, dear reader, four boys taken from the busy life of a great city, place them in the wilderness of Maine, where they had to make a winrow of the forest to secure a garden spot for the house, pry out the stumps and blast the ledges to sow the seed, then ask yourself what should the harvest be?

Father's business required all of his time in New York City, and we were left with two hired men to develop the farm, our brains and muscles, but mine didn't seem to develop worth a cent. I didn't care for the farmer's life. The plow and scythe had no charms for me. My horny, hardened little hand itched and longed to beat the drums that would marshall men to arms.

After eight months of hard work we had cleared up quite a respectable little farm, an oasis in that forest of pines. A new house and barn had been built, also new fences and stone walls, but not much credit for this belonged to me. Soon after we received a letter from father stating that he would be with us in a short time and bring us a new mother and a little step-sister. This was joyous news, the anticipation of a new mother,

and above all a step-sister, inspired us with new ambition. The fences and barn received a coat of white-
wash, the stones were picked out of the road in front
of the house, the wood-pile was repiled and everything put into apple-pie order. We did not know
what day they would arrive. So each day about the
time the stage coach from Belfast should pass the
corners, we would perch ourselves on the fence in front
of the house to watch for it, and when it did come
in sight, wonder if the folks were in it; if they were,
it would turn at the corners and come toward our
house. Day after day passed, and they did not come,
and we had kind of forgotten about it. Finally one day
while we were all busy burning brush, brother Charlie
came rushing towards us shouting, "The stage coach
is coming! The stage is coming!" Well, such a
scampering for the house! We didn't have time to
wash or fix up, and our appearance would certainly
not inspire our city visitors with much paternal pride
or affection; we looked like charcoal burners. Our
faces, hands and clothes were black and begrimed
from the burning brush, but we couldn't help it; we
were obliged to receive and welcome them as we
were. I pulled up a handful of grass and tried to
wipe my face, but the grass being wet, it left
streaks all over it, and I looked more like
a bogie man than anything else. We all
struggled to brush up and smooth our hair, but it
was no use, the stage coach was upon us, the door
opened, father jumped out, and as we crowded
around him, he looked at us in perfect amazement

and with a kind of humiliated expression behind a
pleasant fatherly smile he exclaimed, "Well, well,
you are a nice dirty looking lot of boys. Lizzie,"
addressing his wife and helping her to alight, "This
is our family, a little smoky; I can't tell which is which,
so we'll have to wait till they get their faces washed to
introduce them by their names." But our new
mother was equal to the occasion for coming to each
of us, and taking our dirty faces in her hands, kissed
us, saying at the same time, "Philip, don't you mind,
they are all nice, honest, hard-working boys, and I
know I shall like them, even if this country air has
turned their skins black." At this moment a tiny
voice called, "Please help me out." All the boys
started with a rush, each eager to embrace the
little step-sister. I was there first, and in an
instant, in spite of my dirty appearance, she sprang
from the coach right into my arms; my brothers
struggled to take her from me, but she tightened her
little arms about my neck and clung to me as if I was
her only protector. I started and ran with her, my
brothers in full chase, down the road, over the
stone walls, across the field, around the stumps
with my prize, the brothers keeping up the chase till
we were all completely tired out, and father com-
pelled us to stop and bring the child to the house.
Afterward we took our turns at caressing and ad-
miring her; finally we apologized for our behavior
and dirty faces, listened to father's and mother's congratulations, concluded father's choice for a wife was
a good one, and that our little step-sister was just

exactly as we wanted her to be, and the prospect of a bright, new and happy home seemed to be already realized.

A home is all right
With father and brother,
But darker than night
Without sister and mother.

The war grew more and more serious. Newspapers were eagerly sought; and every word about the struggle was read over and over again. A new call for troops was made, another and still another, and I was all the time fretting and chafing in the corn or potato field, because I was so young and small. I could not work; the fire of patriotism was burning me up. My eldest brother had arrived at the age and required size to fit him for the service; he enlisted and went to the front. This added new fuel to the flame already within me, and one day I threw down the hoe and declared that I would go to the war! I would join my brother at all hazards. My folks laughed at me and tried to dissuade me from so unwise a step, but my mind was made up, and I was bound to enlist. Enlist I did, when I was only fourteen years of age and extremely small for my years, but I thought I would answer for a drummer boy if nothing else. I found that up hill work, however, but I was bound to "get there," and—I did.

It was easy enough to enlist, but to get mustered into the service was a different thing. I tried for eight long weeks. I enlisted in my own town, but was rejected. I enlisted in an adjoining town — rejected, and so on for weeks and weeks. But I did not give up. I owned at the time a little old gray horse and a two-wheeled jumper or "gig," which I had bought with my savings from the sale of "hoop poles," which are small birch and alder trees that grow in the swamps, and used for hoops on lime casks ; at this time they were worth a half a cent a piece delivered. I would work cutting these poles at times when I could do nothing else, pack them on my back to the road, pile them up, till I had a quantity to sell. At length I concluded I had enough to buy me a horse and cart; the pile seemed as big as a house to me, but when the man came along to buy them, he counted out six thousand good ones and rejected nine thousand that were bad. . "Too small!" he said.

"Too small?" I exclaimed, "why there is hardly any difference in them!" But he was buying, I was selling, and under the influence of a boy's anxiety, he paid me thirty dollars, which I counted over and over again, and at every count the dollars seemed to murmer, "A horse, a horse!—war! war! to the front! be a soldier!" I could picture nothing but a soldier's life ; I could almost hear the sounds of the drums, and almost see the long rows of blue-coated soldiers marching in glorious array with steady step to the music of the band. "Thirty! thirty!" I would repeat to myself, but finally concluded thirty wouldn't buy much of a horse, but my heart was set upon it, and nothing remained for me to do but cut more "poles." One day when

I arrived at the road with a bundle of them, a farmer happened to be passing, driving a yoke of oxen as I tumbled my hoop-poles over the fence on to the pile.

"Heow be yer?" Addressing me in a high, nasal twang peculiar to the yeomanry of Maine, and then calling to his oxen without a change of tone, he drawled, "Whoa! back! Whoa you, Turk! Whoa, Bright!" at the same time hitting the oxen over their noses with his goad-stick, and resting on the yoke, he asked, What yer goin' ter dew with them poles?"

"Sell them," I replied.

"What dew yer want for 'em?" taking in the height and width of the pile with a calculating eye.

"Fifty cents a hundred," I said, with some trepidation.

"Don't want nothin', dew yer," coming over and picking out the smallest pole in the pile; "Pooty durned small, been't they? What'll yer take fur the hull lot?"

"Twenty dollars," I said.

"Twenty dollars! Whew!" Emitting a whistle that would have done credit to a locomotive exhausting steam. "Why, thar been't more'n a thousan' thar, be thar?"

"Oh yes, I guess there are over four thousand."

"Say!" sticking his hands in either breeches pocket and taking me in from head to foot with a comprehensive glance, "What might yer name be?"

"Ulmer," I said.

"No? You bcen't Phil's son, be yer?"

"Yes, sir."

"Yer don't tell me! Wall, by gosh! I like Phil, he's a durned smart 'un. I'll tell yer what, I'd like ter see him and Jimmie Blaine a settin' up in them gol-durn presidential chcers; why, by gosh, they'd jist open the hull durned treasury bildin' an let all ther gor-ramed gold an' silver rolc right out in'ter the streets, by gosh, they would." Having delivered himself of this panegyric, together with an accumulated quantity of saliva resulting from the constant mastication of a large tobacco quid, h: again turned his attention to the pile of poles and said, "How much did yer say fur the lot?"

"Twenty dollars."

"Twenty!" Drawing the corners of his mouth down and stroking his chin, then turning to me, "Wall, more I look at yer, by gosh, yer do look like Phil. Wall, I'd like purty well ter have them poles, but—," as if a sudden idea had struck him, — "Don't want ter trade fur a horse, dew yer?"

"What kind of a horse?"

"Wall, a pooty durned good 'un. I hain't druve him much lately, but he yused ter go like smoke; he's a leetle old but, will prick up his ears like a colt when he's a mind ter."

"Well, I do want a horse, if I can trade for one," I said, trying not to show anxiety.

"Say, got time ter get on' ter the waggin an go over to my farm and see him, take dinner with me? Guess, the old woman 'll have enough for both."

Being anxious, I accepted the invitation, and was soon on the way. He pestered me with all kinds of questions; asked all about my family affairs and told me all of his and every other family for miles about. Finally we reached his house, one of those old-fashioned farm houses with several old tumble-down sheds and out-buildings attached, near by an old barn that was once painted red, the shingles had rotted and blown off here and there, so you could see daylight from any portion inside. Scattered about were old wagon boxes, odd wheels, old toothless harrows, plows, a wheelbarrow upside down with the wheel gone, part of an old harness lying across it; bits of harness were hanging on pegs in the barn. Geese, turkeys and chickens were numerous and clucked about as if they were really pleased to see us, and in fact, I discounted or anticipated the looks of the house from the careless dilapidated appearance of every thing around and about the old man's farm.

He finally unyoked his oxen, dropped the yoke right where he took it off and turned his cattle into the yard. "Now then, we'll get a bite to eat, and I'll she⸺ you two horses, and durn me if I won't give you

your choice and a good trade." "Martha-Ann," he
called, "Martha-Ann!"

In a moment a little, bright, bustling old woman
came to the door and shading her eyes with her
apron, called back : "What is it, Dan'l? Did you
bring the merlasses, and candles, and the broom?"

"Yes," he answered back.

"And the salt?"

"Yes."

"And the rennet for the cheese, and the salt-
pork?"

"Yes, yes, yes," he answered, "and I've brought
a young man, Phil. Ulmer's son; goin to trade him
'Dick.'

"What?" said she, coming out to where we
were. "Now, Dan'l, you are not going to do anything of the kind."

"Yes, I be," he said.

"You shan't, I wont have my horse sold; you
know he is the only one I can drive, and he is so
kind and gentle, and the only good horse you have ;
you shan't sell him. And then she sat down on the
cart-tongue and cried as if her heart would break,
and I began to think I was going to really get a
splendid horse at a bargain.

All through the dinner she sobbed, and when she
would pass me bread or anything, it was with a heart-
broken sigh, and I began to want that horse.

Finally dinner finished, he took me to the barn.
There were two horses together standing on the barn-
floor eating corn-husk. They both looked as if they

never had eaten anything else. One was a bay, and
the other a grey ; they were so poor that you could
mistake either for a barrel with half the staves
fallen in.

"Thar, sir, be two fine critters ; you can have
either; this grey one is Dick, the one the old woman
is so sot on, but he's getting too frisky for her ter
handle, he's the best dispositioned animal yer ever
saw; yer do anything with him, he's always ready. Get
him with 'tother on a load at the bottom of a big hill
and he's thar every time; yer see, he's a leetle sprung
in one knee thar, he done that by pulling; it don't
hurt him a bit ter drive, and go! Why, do you know
he's trotted in two minutes? You notice, one eye 's
bit off color! Blue? Wall sir, that was strained a
leetle by watching over his blinder to see that no
other hoss should pass or get near him when he were
druve on the race track twelve years ago, but it don't
hurt him now."

"You praise this horse," I remarked, "but don't
say a word about the other."

"Oh, he don't need it," said the old man dryly.

I was so anxious to get a horse, I concluded to
take Dick. I thought, he must be the best on
Martha-Ann's account, and really there didn't seem
much choice.

"You want a harness and waggin too, don't yer?"

"Yes," I replied, "I shall have to have something to drive him in."

"Wall, I guess I can fix you out with a full rig."

So after looking through the sheds, he pulled out

an old gig with one shaft broken and without wheels.
"Guess I'll find the wheels of this somewhar. Do
you know this is the same gig that very Dick yused
ter haul on the race track ; he may remember it after
yer hitch him into it. If he does, you want to look
out for him, and here are the wheels."

He pulled them out of a pile of old lumber and
rubbish, and fitted them on; one was badly dished in
and was painted red, the other was as badly dished
out and one day had been painted yellow; but I was
anxious and didn't object ; I wanted to get home.

So after getting the "gig" together, he patched
a harness from the odd pieces he found, then fitted
them on to the poor horse who looked as if he was
sorry he was alive.

Finally we had everything all ready. I mounted
the "gig." As I did so, I noticed it seemed one sided,
and looking at the wheels, I found one was somewhat
larger than the other, but said nothing. Taking up
the lines made up my mind to get home and fix it
there. I pulled on the reins and spoke to "Dick,"
but he didn't move. The old man took him by
the bridle and led him to the road remarking at
the same time, "Dick never did like to go away from
home."

After we reached the road, the old man hit "Dick"
with a hoe handle, and off he started. It was four miles
from his house to ours, and I reached home NEXT DAY.
Figured up what the whole thing cost me: The horse
stood me $33.50, the "gig" $7.50, and the harness, (?)
75 cents. This was my outfit to make or break me.

My brothers laughed at my trade, but I didn't care,
I had a purpose, and I was bound to accomplish it.

When I wanted to use my "rig," to harness the
horse, I was obliged to take a ladder to put his bridle
on, lead him alongside of the steps to put the saddle
and breeching on, and back him up to the well-curb
to put his tail in the "crupper," and after he was
hitched to the "gig," nine times out of ten he would
wait till he was ready to go.

Some time after I learned that uncle "Dan'l"
was a regular horse dealer and kept just such old
plugs around him, and that they were always his wife's
favorites when the old man wanted to get one off his
hands.   However, Dick and I became great friends.
I fixed up the old "gig," and it answered my purpose.
I got there with it.

It became a customary daily routine for me to
harness this poor animal, start at sundown and drive
all night.   Where?   Why to Augusta to try and get
mustered in, but I would always ride back broken
hearted and disappointed, my ardor, however, not
dampened a bit.   I became a guy to my brothers and
neighbors.   My father and step-sister indulged me in
my fancy, helping me all they could—father by fur-
nishing me with money, and step-sister by putting up
little lunches for my pilgrimages during the night.
They thought me partially insane, and judged it
would be best to let me have my own idea, with the
hope that it would soon wear off.   But it didn't.
I would not give up.   The Yankee yearning for fight
had possession of me, and I could neither eat, sleep

nor work. I was bound to be a soldier. I prayed
for it, and I sometimes thought, my prayers were
answered; that the war should last 'till I was big
enough to be one—for it did.

I had enlisted four times in different towns, and
each time I went before a mustering officer, I was
rejected. "Too small" I was every time pronounced,
but I was not discouraged or dismayed—the indomitable pluck and energy of those downeast boys per-
vaded my system. I was bound to get there, for what
I didn't know, I did not care or didn't stop to think. I
only thought of the glory of being a soldier, little
realizing what an absurd-looking one I would make;
but the ambition was there, the pluck was there, and
the patriotism of a man entered the breast of the wild
dreamy boy. I wanted to go to the front—and I went.

After several unsuccessful attempts to be mustered into the service at Augusta, which was twenty-
five miles from our little farm, I thought I would enlist
from the town of Freedom and thereby get before a
different mustering officer who was located in Belfast.
I had grown, I thought, in the past six weeks, and
before a new officer, I thought my chances of
being accepted would improve; so on a bright morning in September I mounted my "gig," behind my
little old gray horse, who seemed to say, as he
turned his head to look at me when I jumped on to
the seat, "What a fool you are, making me haul you
all that distance, when you know they won't have
you!" but kissing my little step-sister good-bye, with
a wave of my hand to father and brothers who

stood in the yard and door of the dear old home, I
drove away, and as I did so I could see the expres-
sions of ridicule and doubt on their faces, while un-
derneath it all there was a tinge of sadness and fear.
They did not think for a moment. I would be mustered
into the army, yet fear took possession of them when
I drove off, for they knew my determined disposition.

Well, I arrived in Belfast. Instead of driving
direct to the stable and hotel, and putting my horse
up, I drove direct to the office of the mustering officer.
I did not need to fasten my trusty horse, for he knew
it would only be a few moments, and as I went to the
office door, he turned his head and whinnied as if he
were laughing at me. I entered that office like a
young Napoleon. I had made up my mind to walk
in before the officer very erect and dignified, even to
raising myself on tiptoe. On telling the clerk my
errand, he ushered me into an inner office, and imagine my surprise—my consternation—when, swinging
around in his chair, I found myself in the presence of
the very officer who had rejected me in Augusta so
many times.

"Damn it," said he, "will you never let up? Go
home to your mother, boy, don't pester me any more.
I will not accept you, and let that end it."

I tremblingly told him "I had grown since he saw
me last, and that by the time I was mustered in I
would grow some more, and that I would drum and
fight, if it should prove actually necessary."

Thus I pleaded with him for fully one hour.
Finally he said, "Well, damned if I don't muster

you in, just to get rid of you. Sergeant, make out
this young devil's papers and let him go and get
killed." My heart leaped into my mouth. I tried to
thank him, but he would not have it. He hurried me
through, and at 5:30 P. M., September 15, 1863, I
was a United States soldier. And when I donned
that uniform, what a looking soldier! The smallest
clothes they issued looked on me as if it would
make a suit for my entire family, but in spite of the
misfit, I took them and put them on, with the pants legs
rolled up to the knees, and the overcoat dragging on
the ground.

I went out of that office as proud as a peacock,
but a laughing-stock for the boys, and all who gazed
at me. I think even the old horse smiled and looked
askance; he acted as if I was fooling him, and hungry
as he was, when he turned towards the stable, he
dragged along as if he either were sorry or ashamed
to draw me among people ; but I cared not for their
jeers and laughs. I was now a soldier and anxious to
get home. I pictured the feeling and joyous greet-
ings of my brothers and sister as they would see me
ride up in my uniform; how the boys would envy me,
and how the sister would throw her arms about me
and kiss me, and how her bosom would heave with
pride as she gazed upon the uniform that covered her
hero brother. Oh! I pictured it all in my boyish
fancy, and hastened all my arrangements, so full of
joy that I could scarcely eat. I would not wait till
morning, but started home about midnight, arriving
there just at sunrise.

It was on the 17th of September, 1863, one of those bright, balmy days that we have in good old New England, seated in a "gig," might be seen the writer of this little sketch, dressed in soldiers' clothes, covered by one of those familiar cape overcoats that nearly covered the "gig" and poor old horse. I felt as proud as if I was the general in command of all the army.

Instead of giving the family a surprise, they had heard of my enlisting from the stage-driver, and I found them all in tears. But when I made my appearance tears changed to laughter, for the sight of me I think was enough to give them hope. They didn't believe our government would have such a little, ill-dressed soldier. And father said, after looking me all over: "Well, if they have mustered you in, after they see you in that uniform it will be muster out, my boy."

In about ten days I received orders to report in Augusta. Then the family realized there was more in it than they at first thought, but consoled them-

selves with the belief that when I reached headquarters, I would be found useless, and sent home.
I went away, leaving them with that feeling of hope
struggling behind their copious tears. And the linger-
ing kiss of my little step-sister, and her soft sobbing,
"Don't, don't, please don't go," as she hung around
my neck, ran constantly in my mind from that time
till now. All through the nights, on the long
marches, in all my troubles, that soft, sweet voice
was calling, "George, please, please, don't go."
And I could see her little form, and her ever-thought-
ful face, a guiding star and a compass that ever
guided me away from the shoals and quicksands.
She was an angel companion to me all through the
trials and hardships of that awful war.

Well, I arrived in Portland, was sent to the barracks with three or four thousand others, was allotted
a hard bunk, and then for the first time did I realize
what I was doing, what I had committed myself to,
and I think if I could have caught that mustering
officer I should have appealed to him just as hard to
muster me out, as I did to muster me in ; but I was
in it and must stay. I will never forget the first day
of my soldier experience. With what feeling of awe
and thumping of my cowardly, timid heart, I heard
the different commands of the officers. The disciplin-
ing began ; the routine of a soldier's life had really
started right in Portland, far away from the front
where I had only expected to find it. I was detained
in those barracks only a few days, and the tap of the
drum, and the sound of the bugle as they sounded

their different calls, had grown monotonous to me ; I
no longer regarded them with awe, but with mockery.
I wanted to go to the front where the real life of a
soldier was known, where glory could be won.   I
wanted the reality, not boy's play.

I was glad when I was numbered among a squad
of about 200 who had orders to go to Washington.
That night we marched down to the depot and were
crowded into cars. I did not care; I was overjoyed ;
I was delighted at the prospects of going to
the seat of war, near the front, where I thought
I might hear the booming of the cannon, and to
a place where I would soon be forwarded to my
regiment.   We arrived in Boston, and to my dis-
appointment, were laid over.   We were marched to the
barracks on Beach street, which in early days was
the "Beach Street Theater."   The seats, benches,
gallery, stage and scenery were all there, and we
were crowded into this old, unused temple of Thespis
to select a place to sleep where best we could, on the
floor, or anywhere.   Here I began to grow sick of
soldiering ; we were in this old musty theater with a
guard over us, not allowed to go on the street, and
unable to find out how long we were to be incarcerated there, for we were treated more like prisoners
than men who had volunteered to serve their country.

I thought it a great hardship at that time, and
kicked at it loud and hard, without any result that ben-
efited us; but since I have been through it all, I can see
where it was absolutely necessary to use the rigid and
seemingly ungrateful discipline.   Well, we were kept

in the old theater for about a week; we were allowed
out for two hours each day on passes, and in the evening we sang songs and "acted" on the stage.   Each
one who could recite or do anything did it, and it was
appreciated by a deadhead audience, something un-
usual nowadays.   It was here in this old Beach
Street Theater that my future life was undoubtedly
mapped out ; from that time I was impressed with a
desire to become an actor, and there is no doubt that
the seed was planted then and grew and increased in
after years.

On the 11th of November, we were ordered to
Washington, and embarked on the steamboat train
via Fall River, and I shall never forget when we
arrived in New York, the demonstration, the greet-
ing, the cheers, the God-speeds that we received as
we marched through the city to the ferry, and it .
seemed to me that I was the one all this was meant
for ; I thought I was a hero.   It seemed that all eyes
were on me, and perhaps they were, for among all
those Maine giants I belied my state, for I was a dot
only, a pigmy beside those mighty woodsmen.

We arrived in Washington without mishap.   I
was granted permission to go over the city, and then
to report to the commanding officer of the camp at
Alexandria.   My first desire when I found myself
with a privilege in the great capital was to visit President Lincoln, have a talk with him and also with
Secretary Stanton.   My admiration for those two
men was almost love, and I fancied, now that I was a
soldier. that I could easily meet them ; that they

Our Troops Passing Through Washington to the Front.

would grasp me by the hand, compliment and shower
me with congratulations and advice. It is needless to
say that I found out that I had overestimated my importance ; I did not discuss the war situation with
either of those gentlemen. I was a little crestfallen
at not meeting them, but contented myself by looking
over the city ; and wherever I went I noticed I was
scrutinized by everybody ; soldiers on guard would
come to a halt, hesitate and then present arms ; some
officers would pass me by, then turn and look me
over from head to foot ; others would touch their
caps and then turn and watch me with a kind of wondering gaze, as much as to say, "What is it?"

I forgot to mention that while in Portland
I had a tailor make me a very handsome suit of military clothes. He was as ignorant of the regulation
style as I was. He only knew the colors and knew
that I wanted it nice and handsome. He made it and
so covered it over with gold braid and ornaments,
that you could not tell whether I was a drum-major
or a brigadier-general ; that accounted for the saluta-
tions and looks of astonishment I received.

The first night I was tired out and started for
Alexandria ; arrived at headquarters about midnight,
and told the sentry I must see the colonel. He
thought I had important messages, or was some
officer, and escorted me to the colonel's quarters. I
woke him up, told him I had reported and wanted
a bed.

The colonel said, "Is that all you want? Cor-
poral, put this man in the guard-house." He did!

That was my first experience, and I always after tried to avoid guard-houses. The next morning I was given a broom and put to sweeping around camp with about twenty tough-looking customers. The broom did not look well with my uniform, and as soon as an officer noticed me, I was summoned before the colonel in command. He asked, what I was? I told him I didn't know yet—would not know 'till I reached my regiment. He had a hearty laugh at my appearance; said I ought to be sent to some fair instead of the front. However, he detailed me as his orderly. I held this position some time, until one day there was going to be a squad of recruits, and returned furloughed men sent on a steam-barge to the front at City Point, where Butler was bottled up. I asked to be one of them. The colonel told me I was foolish, and better stay with him, but I insisted ; and he allowed me to go. The barge was a kind of an open double-deck boat without cabin or shelter, and they crowded us on to her as thick as we could stand ; we were like sardines. I secured a position against the smoke-stack, and before we reached Chesapeake bay I was glad of it, for it became bitterly cold, and I curled down around this smoke-stack, went to sleep, and when I awoke in the morning I was crisp, dirty, and nearly roasted alive. We crossed the bay in the afternoon. Oh, wasn't it rough! This old river barge would roll and pitch out of sight at times, and we were all wet from head to foot. Then I began to wish myself home on the farm again ; but I was in for it, and could not back out. I had one thought that buoyed me up, the thought of meeting my brother.

That evening we passed by Fortress Monroe, up the James river. There was not much transpired to relieve the monontony or appease our hunger or thirst ; in fact, it began to look dubious as to reaching City Point. The monotony, however, was somewhat relieved in the morning. About daylight a commotion˙ was caused by the sound of distant cannonading. Every one crowded to the front of the boat; everybody was asking questions of everybody. Each one had some idea to offer as to the cause. Some ventured to say it was a gunboat up the river practising. One old chap, who had evidently been to the front, facetiously claimed that it was the corks out of Butler's bottles. The river was very crooked at this point, and you could not see very far ; but presently we rounded a bend in the river, which revealed to us where the cannonading came from, but for what, we could not make out. About a mile ahead of us lay a United States gunboat, and every few minutes a puff of smoke, and then a loud bang— erang—erang—erang—with its long vibrations on that still morning, awoke a sense of fear in everyone aboard that boat. No one could account for the situation. Even the captain of the barge stood with pallid cheek, seemingly in doubt what to do as he rang the bell to slow down ; but on—on we kept moving—nearer and nearer this most formidable war-ship, and as we did so the shots became more frequent. Then we noticed a man on the bank waving a flag back and forth, up

and down in a wild, excited sort of a way. I asked
what that meant. An old soldier said the man was
signaling the boat to let them know they had hit
the target.

Suddenly we were brought to an understand-
ing of what it all meant, for we could now hear the
musketry very plain, and could even see the rebels
on the banks of the river. At this point a "gig"
from the gunboat pulled alongside and gave orders
to the captain "to land those troops at once," telling
him at the same time that this was Fort Powhatan
landing; that Fitzhugh Lee with his cavalry had
swooped down upon the garrison, which was only
composed of two hundred negro troops, and that
they must be re-enforced. The captain protested, as
the troops on board were all unarmed, being returned
furloughed men and recruits ; but it was no use, the
order was imperative, and the captain headed his
barge toward the shore. There was no wharf. That
had been burnt, so he was obliged to run as far as
he could onto the sand, then land us overboard. I
tell you as that boat neared toward the shore, my
face felt as if it were marbleized ; sharp twinges ran
up and down my whole body, and I'll bet that I was
the picture of a coward. I was not the only one. I
looked them all over, every one looked just as I felt.
One man who stood near me, I know, was more
frightened than I, for he was so frightened he smelt
badly. But I didn't blame any of those poor men;
it was not the pleasantest thing in the world to be

Battle between Monitor and Merrimack off Fortress Monroe.

placed before the enemy as we were. However, we
all landed.

The firing above us on the bank became more
intense. An officer who was on the boat with us,
returning from a leave of absence, assumed command.
He ordered us to fall into line, and marched us into a
little ravine, halted, and told us the position and
necessity of the occasion. He said the fort was a
very important position, and must be held at all
hazards ; that there were only two hundred colored
troops there, and they could not hold it. Now, he
proposed, as we had no arms, to go in with a rush
and a yell, and make those rebels think that re-enforcements had arrived. All this time the musketry firing
was increasing. The whizz of bullets through the air
and about our heads were becoming too frequent. I
was in the front rank, center of the line, and I tell
you I think I had a little of that frightened smell about
me at this time. Whether it was that or my looks or
what, the officer probably took pity on me and told
me to skirmish in the rear. I hardly knew where the
rear was, but I thought it would be safer under the
bank of the river, and there I hastened, and none too
soon, for the rebels had made a break through the
lines and poured several volleys into our poor, unarmed re-enforcements. The rebs became more cau-
tious, and that was what was wanted, as the only
hope we had was to hold them at bay until re-enforcements could arrive.

Well, I skirmished in the rear, and I found it
hotter than the front, for the rebs would crawl to the

bank at either end of the breastworks and kept a
cross-fire up and down the river.   Under and against
the banking, there was a sort of old barn ; this was
filled with hay.   The bullets were flying around so
thickly that I squeezed myself behind this barn, and
after I was well in, the bullets just rained against that
old building ; but I felt pretty secure till I looked up
overhead—I saw that while I was in safety from
bullets, a worse danger threatened me.   The over-
hanging bank was liable to cave in and bury me alive.

The uncertainty of my position became more
and more apparent.   Each moment the increased
storm of bullets on the barn prevented me from even
looking out, and the constant rattling down of dirt
and pebbles from above, told me plainly what a position I was in.   I tell you I wished then I had never been
mustered in.   The uncertainty of my position was
soon developed.   I came to myself and found I was
buried to my neck ; my head and face were cut and
bleeding, and a soldier was trying to wipe the sand
from my eyes and ears.   I found I had not been shot,
but the banking had caved in and buried me.   Gen.
"Baldy" Smith, who was in command, happened to see
me behind the barn just as the bank caved in.   It was
he who put the soldiers at work to rescue me.   As
soon as I was out, and the dust out of my eyes, the
general rode down to the beach, leading an extra
horse ; he called to me.   Ordered me to mount.   I
did so.   He made me his orderly.

A new danger.   I was to carry dispatches across
the field, but I did not now have the fear I did at

first. I did not mind the sound of the bullets. I
became accustomed to it, and I rode back and
forth all day long without a scratch. I believe
I was so small that I rode between those bullets, and from that time forth I had no fear. I
felt as though I were bullet-proof. I felt as if
it were ordained that I should go through the
war unscathed and unscarred. It did seem so, for I
would go through places where it rained bullets, and
come out without a scratch. This was my experience
all through, and was commented on by comrades,
who said I had a charmed life. Well, the day wore
away the rebs making feints first at one point, then
another. Finally they concentrated their forces
against one point, and would have carried it, too, but
just then a steamboat loaded with troops rounded the
bend of the river. Well, the shouts that went up
from the handful of brave soldiers at the sight of
that boat I never can forget. The boys on the boat
caught the sound. They took in the situation, and
answered back the shout with three long, hearty
cheers. It created consternation in the rebel lines.
They knew the jig was up, but they drew up
in line, like dare-devils that they were, and with a
cool deliberation, poured volley after volley into the
side of the steamer until her nose touched the shore.
Well, to see those soldiers leave that steamer was a
sight never to be forgotten. They jumped overboard
from every part of her. It did not seem five minutes
from the time she touched shore until the banks were
swarming with our boys in blue. The rebels had

taken to flight—our boys followed some distance, and
then returned, relieving us and allowing us to embark
again for City Point.   After the rebels had retreated,
I went outside the breastworks, and the sight that met
my eyes on every side would curdle the blood of
stouter hearts than mine.   It appeared that Lee, with
his cavalry, had surprised the pickets, and being
negroes, every one they captured they would hang up
to a tree after they were mutilated.   I saw several
with fingers cut off in order to obtain a ring quickly,
and many other sickening sights which tended to
make me a hardened soldier.   I was having lots of
experience, even before I had really reached my regiment, and I tell you, the heroic ardor of my boyish
dream was beginning to ooze out of me quite fast.   I
began to think I was not cut for a soldier.

Well, my first battle was over, my first experience before an enemy.   The first sound of musketry
had died away, and we were again steaming towards
City Point to join our regiments.   We arrived there
the next night about ten o'clock.   There didn't seem
to be any one in command of us or any one to direct
us.   It was very dark on shore, but in the distance
you could see a glaring light above the horizon, as if
there was a long building on fire.   But from the
occasional sound of guns from that quarter, I made
up my mind it was the advance line of our army.   It
was Butler's command, and our regiment, the Eighth
Maine, must be there.   The Eighth Maine, Company
H, was the regiment and company to which my
brother belonged, and in which I was enlisted.   I

started out across the fields in the direction of the light—on, on I tramped, into ditches, through mires, over fences. The farther I went the faster I went. I was so impatient I could not hold myself to a walk ; it was a dog-trot all the time. I was heedless of every obstacle, till I began to near the front. I realized the danger by the whizzing of shell, and the zip, zip of bullets. I found myself among lots of soldiers, and how ragged and dirty the poor fellows looked. I asked the first man I came to where the Eighth Maine was? He looked at me in perfect astonishment. ''This is the Eighth, what's left of it." I asked him if he knew where my brother was— Charley Ulmer? ''Oh, yes," he said, and pointing to a little group of men, who were round a wee bit of a fire; ''there he is, don't you know him?"

I hesitated, for really I could hardly tell one from the other. He saw my bewilderment, and took me by the arm and led me over to the fire. They all started and stared at me, and to save my life I could not tell which was my brother ; but one more ragged than the rest uttered a suppressed cry, rushed forward, and throwing his arm about my neck, sobbed and cried like a child. ''My God! my brother! Oh George, George, why did you come here?" His grief seemed to touch them all, for they all began to wipe their eyes with their ragged coat-sleeves. This began to tell on me, and for the next ten minutes it was a kind of a blubbering camp. After awhile they reconciled themselves, and began to ply me with questions faster than I could answer. My brother sat down with me and lectured me very soundly for coming, as there was no need of it. He gave a graphic description of the hardships they had endured, and I can never obliterate the picture he presented that night. His clothes were ragged and patched, begrimed with smoke, grease and dirt; his hat an old soft one, with part of the rim gone and the crown perforated with bullet holes; his beard scraggly and dirty; his big toes peeping out of a pair of old boots with the heels all run down, in fact, he was a sight—a strong contrast to my tailor-made suit. I will never forget the expression on my brother's face when about half an hour after my arrival he looked up to me with his eyes half full of tears glistening on that dirty face, and with a kind of cynical smile, asked, after looking me over and over: "What are you, anyhow?"

I told him I didn't know.

"Well, after you have been here awhile, those pretty clothes won't look as they do now, and you will probably find out what you are after you have dodged a few shells."

Our conversation was brought to a climax by orders to break camp and fall in. We learned we were going to embark somewhere on a boat; everything was hustle-bustle now; little sheltered tents were struck, tin cups, canteens, knapsacks were made ready, and in about fifteen minutes that begrimed, dirty, hungry family of Uncle Sam's was on the march to the river. We were marched on board an old ferry-boat, and crowded so thickly that we could scarcely stand. My brother seemed now to feel that he had the responsibility of my comfort, even my life, on his hands—and being a favorite he elbowed me a place at the end of the boat, where we could sit down by letting our feet hang over the end of the boat. In that position we remained. We didn't have room to stand up and turn around. I was awful sleepy, but dared not go to sleep for fear I would fall overboard. Finally my brother fixed me so I could lay my head back, and he held on to me while I slept. The next morning we landed at a place called West Point, on the York river; why we landed there we didn't know. Of course soldiers never did know anything of the whys and wherefores; they only obeyed orders, stood up or laid down and got killed—they had no choice in the matter. Well, we landed, and I tell you, we were stiff and hungry. While they were unloading the horses, which was done by lowering them into the water and letting them swim ashore, which took some time, they allowed us a chance to skirmish for food. About half a mile from the river were a dozen houses—nice-looking places. Towards these we started; they were all closed up; they all looked deserted; there was not a sign of life, except the cackle of hens or chickens in the hen-house. Chickens were good enough for us, and I was one of the first to get to the pen; secured two handfuls of chicks, and was just emerging with them when a big woman confronted me; she stood and looked me straight in the eye,

and with both hands held on to a mastiff, that to me
looked as big as an ox.

"How dare you?" said she.

"I don't," said I.

"What are you doing with my chickens, you
good-for-nothing Yankee thief?"

I tried to apologize, but it was no use. Even
my pretty uniform had no more effect than my elo-
quence. I simply put Mr. and Mrs. Chicks down
and backed out of the yard. She was good enough
to hold on to the dog, for which I was very grateful.
I think I had more respect for the dog than the lady.
However, I had to resort to pork and hard tack for my
breakfast. About noon that day we began our march.
Where we were going, everbody guessed, but none
knew. I didn't care. I was now a kind of a half-
settled soldier, but from the first, I was a kind of
privileged character. No one gave me orders. No
one seemed to claim me. I had never been assigned
to any company. I never had to answer roll-call. I
could go and come as I pleased. Once in awhile a
guard would halt me, but not often. They didn't
know what I was, and they didn't care. All the afternoon we marched. Our route was along the railroad,
the rails of which had the appearance of being
recently torn up by the rebels. About four o'clock
I was becoming very tired. We came to a clearing,
and some distance in the field was a darky plowing
with a mule. I made a break for him, and the rest
of that march I rode. No one objected, but the boys
shouted as I made my appearance on the mule; a

mile or two further along we sighted a farm-house.
I drew reins on my mule and made for the house ; I
made the boys glad on my return, for I secured a
demijohn of applejack, a big bundle of tobacco, and
a box of eggs. That successful raid gave me courage, and I began to think that was what I was
destined for, and I liked it first-rate, for it was a
pleasure to me to see those poor, hungry boys have
any delicacy, or even enough of ordinary food.

That night we had to halt, for the rebs had
burned the bridge, and we had to wait for pontoons.
The boys were tired and hungry. A guard was
posted to prevent any foraging, but I was a privileged character, and I bolted through the lines. I
had seen some pigs and calves scamper into the
swamp about half a mile back from where we halted,
and thinking a bit of fresh meat would be nice for the
boys, I determined to have some. Cautiously I
stole away, till I arrived at the edge of the swamp ;
and such a jungle! It was almost impossible to pen-
etrate it, so I skirted the edge, hoping to see a
pig emerge. After tramping an hour I was rewarded
by seeing a calf. I drew my revolver, sneaked up
and fired at poor bossy. It dropped—I was a good
shot—but when I reached the poo꞉ ꞉ ast I found it
was as poor as a rail and covered with sores as big as
my hand. I was disappointed, but cut off as much
as I could that was not sore, and took it to camp.
We put the kettles on the fires in short order, and my
brother's company had fresh meat broth—the first
fresh meat in a month—and I tell you it was good,

even if it had been sore.   After that episode Company H claimed me and dubbed me their mascot.   I
accepted the position, and from that time forth I
devoted my time to foraging, stealing anything I
could for my company, and I doubt if there was a
company in the whole army that fared better than
ours, for I was always successful in my expeditions.

After a long, tedious march across pontoons,
over corduroy roads, we confronted the Johnnies at
"Cold Harbor."   It was here that I found myself in a
real, genuine battle.   I got lost in the scuffle.   I
found myself amidst bursting shell and under heavy
musketry fire.   I was bewildered and frightened.   I
did not know which way to go.   I ran this way and
that, trying to find my brother and regiment.   Every
turn I made it seemed I encountered more bullets
and shells.   Soldiers were shouting and running in
every direction, artillery was galloping here and
there, on every side it seemed they were fighting for
dear life.   On one side of me I saw horses and men
fall and pile up on top of each other.   Cannon and
caissons with broken wheels were turned upside
down, riderless horses were scampering here and
there, officers were riding and running in all directions, the shells were whizzing through the air, and
soldiers shouting at the top of their voices.   Everything seemed upside down.   I thought the world had
come to an end.   I tried to find shelter behind a tree,
away from the bullets, but as soon as I found shelter
on one side it seemed as though the bullets and shells
came from all sides, and I lay down in utter despair

Desperate Charge of Confederates to Capture a Union Battery.

and fright. I don't know how long I was there, but
when I awoke I thought the war was over, it was so
still. I thought every one had been killed on both
sides, excepting myself. I was just thinking I would
try and find a live horse, ride back to Washington
and tell them that the war was over, everybody was
killed, when my brother tapped me on the shoulder
and asked me where I had been. He had gone
through it all, escaped with the loss of one toe, and
had come to the rear to have it dressed and find me.

The next morning I was sent with the "Stretcher
Corps" under a flag of truce to the battle field to help

take the wounded to the rear and bury the dead, and
when we reached the scene, how well could I imagine
what the awful struggle had been. The worst of the
great conflict had occurred in an orchard, and there
the sight was most appalling; dead and dying heroes
were lying about as thick as a slumbering camp
would be, sleeping with their guns for pillows the
night before a battle ; to many of those poor fellows
it was that sleep that knows no waking, while to
others it was the awaking from unconsciousness by the
twinges of a mortal gaping wound, awake just long
enough to get a glimpse of the Gates Ajar, sink back
and start on that journey from which no traveler
returns.

Blue and the gray were mingled together on this
awful field of slaughter, and both sides seemed to respect the solemnity by a cessation of hostilities, and
the hushed silence was only broken by the painful cry
of some helpless wounded, or dying groans of others.
The little white cloth we wore around our arms to
denote, we belonged to the stretcher corps, seemed
to add to the sadness of the occasion, for to those
poor wounded souls we were like ministering
angels, and as I moved from one to the other with
tear dimmed eyes offering water and assistance to those
who needed it I saw many incidents of bravery and
self-sacrifice that went far toward ameliorating the
suffering and obliterating the bitterness of the blue
and the gray. I noticed one poor fellow who had
spread his rubber blanket to catch the dew of the
night sharing the moisture thus gathered with an

unfortunate confederate who had lost a leg. Another, a confederate was staying the life-blood of a union officer by winding his suspenders around the mangled limb. Oh! the horror of such a picture can never be penned—or told, and contemplated only by soldiers who have been there.

One-half of our regiment had been killed or wounded. After this things settled down into a siege. I employed my time foraging for the company. One day I found an apple orchard, gathered as many apples as I could carry, took them to the company and made apple-sauce without sweetening. They ate very heartily of it, poor fellows. It was a treat for them; but it was a bad find, for the next day the whole lot of them were unfit for duty. That nearly put a stop to my reconnoitering. Our regiment lay here in the advance line of breastworks for thirteen days. The sappers and miners were constantly working our breastworks towards the enemy, and every time I wanted to reach my company I found it in a new place and more difficult to reach. The rebel sharpshooters, with their deadly aim, were waiting for such chaps as me. However, under cover of night, I always managed to find and reach the company with some palatable relish.

I will never forget one night; four men were detailed to go to the rear for rations. The commissary was located about two miles to the rear, and the wagon could only haul the rations within one mile of us on account of jungle and rebel sharpshooters. Therefore these men were detailed to pack the rations the rest of the way. I was one of the detail from my company. We went back to the covered wagons that were waiting for us. The boys said I was too small to walk, and they threw me into the rear end of one of the wagons. We got to the commissary tent— a long tent open at both ends—and from both ends they weighed out the rations of coffee, sugar, etc. While the soldier who was doing the weighing on one end had his back turned, I managed to fill my haversack from a full barrel of coffee that stood at the end of the tent. I had two haversacks for that purpose, for I went there with that intent ; but I came away with only one filled. I could not get a chance for the other ; it was on the wrong side. Finally the rations were all aboard, and we started back. The boys repeated the operation of throwing me into the wagon again, and there was my opportunity. I would fill my other haversack from the bags in the wagon ; that's what the boys expected I would do, and I did from the first bag I could get into. Each company had its own bag.

When we arrived at the breastworks my company crowded around me for plunder. I divided it up, and was looked upon as quite a hero, but when the rations were issued it was found our company's bag was short about thirty rations of sugar, but no one said a word. It was surmised that it got spilled. Day after day our regiment lay there and our army did not seem to gain anything. I was becoming disgusted and discouraged.

One night the Johnnies made a charge on us. That was the only time I ever fired a gun in the whole war, and I honestly believe I killed a dozen men, for immediately after they stopped firing. It was only a few moments, however; on they came, only to be repulsed. They kept that up nearly all night, and I served my country by standing down in the trench, loading a gun and passing it up to my brother to fire. I did this all night, but I didn't see any less rebels in the morning. Our next order was to fall back, under cover of darkness. We fell back about a mile and halted for some reason, I thought to get breakfast. Anyway I built a little fire behind a stone wall, put my coffee-pot on and the remnants of a pot of beans. They were getting nice and hot; my brother and I stood waiting, smacking our lips in the anticipation of a feast, when whizz came one of those nasty little "Cohorn" mortor shells and it dropped right into our coffee and beans. Then the bugle sounded, "fall in," and we started with downcast hearts and empty stomachs, and a longing good-bye to the debris of beans and coffee. It was a tiresome march. Of course, we didn't know where we were going, and that made it all the longer.

We eventually brought up at White-House landing on the York river, where we were put on board of a steam transport without being given time to draw rations. From there we steamed down the York and up the James river to the Appomattox, and up the river to Point of Rocks. We landed here on the Bermuda Hundred side, in the rear of Butler's

works, obtained some bread and coffee, and then
crossed the Appomattox on pontoons and pushed on
towards Petersburg. Our regiment belonged at that
time to the 2nd brigade, 2nd division of the 18th
corps, commanded by Major General "Baldy" Smith.

We soon met the enemy's pickets in front of
Petersburg. They fled before that long, serpentine
file of blue-coats like deer. On, on we went. We
could see the rebels running in their shirt sleeves,
throwing coats, guns and everything in their mad flight.
I don't think there was a shot fired on either side 'till
we reached a fort, Smith I think it was called. It
was just at dusk. This fort was located on a mound
or hill with a ravine in front of it. Our brigade was
drawn up in line of battle in a wheat-field on the right.
A colored brigade was ordered to charge the fort
from the hill opposite, and across this ravine ; then I
beheld one of the grandest and most awful sights I ever
saw; those colored troops started on a double quick,
and as they descended the hill, the fort poured volley
after volley into them. The men seemed to fall like
blades of grass before a machine, but it did not stop
them; they rallied and moved on; it was only the
work of a few minutes. With a yell they were up and
into that fort, and in less time than it takes to tell it,
the guns were turned on the fleeing rebels. Here
was the greatest mistake of our greatest commander.
All of our army was brought to a standstill by some
one's foolish order. Not another move was made.
We lay there waiting, and all night long we could
hear the trains rumbling along on the other side of the

Appomattox river. Lee had been outwitted. We had
stolen a march on him. We had arrived in front of
defenseless Petersburg, and could have gone right in
and on to Richmond without a struggle. But that
fatal order to halt gave him all night to hurry his forces
from Cold Harbor, and in the morning we found
plenty of determined rebels in front of us, and thereby
the war was prolonged months and hundreds and thousands of lives lost. I swore all night. I kicked and
condemned every general there was in the army for
the blunder I saw they were making. I only wished
I could be the general commanding for one hour. But
it was no use; I couldn't be.

I was nothing but a boy. But I had my ideas.
I thought, perhaps, more than some of the officers
did. I kept myself posted on facts and the topog-
raphy of the country. The dispositions of generals
was a matter of grave importance to me. I believed
generals should be selected to command, NOT for their
qualifications in military tactics alone, NOT because
they had graduated well-dressed from "West Point,"
but for their indomitable pluck, judgment and honesty
of purpose. It did seem to me that some of our best
officers were invariably placed in the most unimportant positions and commands. Take, for instance,
"Custer's" Brigade of daring men, headed by those
intrepid officers, Alger and Towns, wasting their time
and imperiling the lives of thousands of good soldiers
around "Emettsburg," "Gordonsville," "Bottom
Bridge," carrying out the foolish orders of superiors
in command. Why could not these officers of cool

judgment be with us at this critical moment?—they made THEIR victories, what would they have done had they the great opportunities that were presented to others who failed?

All night about the camp-fire the boys would delight in nagging me—getting me into arguments and debates. They called me the ''midget orator of the Army of the Potomac.'' I will never forget one night soon after the advance on Petersburg ; we were clustered about with coffee cups and pipes ; an argument waxed warm in regard to the possibilities of the war lasting two more years ; finally I was called upon for my views. ''Midget,'' said Col. McArthur, ''if you had supreme command of our army, what would you do?''

What would I do? If Uncle Sam would give me one regiment from each State in the Union—give me Grant, Burnside, Sherman, Sheridan, Custer, Alger, Hooker, Hancock, Thomas and Siegel to command them, I would take Richmond and settle the rebellion before they had time to wire and ask Stanton if I should. This was received with cheering and applause. But my boyish fancies and ideas were never gratified ; I never had the pleasure of seeing my ideal army together, and Richmond was not taken for many months afterward.

A few days after our regiment was drawn up in line of battle in a wheatfield. It was just nightfall. I was lying down on the bank of a ditch waiting for the move-forward. Suddenly a shell came over my

head and bust right in the center of my company. I
thought I saw legs and arms flying in all directions.

I started on the dead run for the rear. I believed
I was going right, but it seemed as if the shells were
coming from our own guns in the rear. I thought
they had mistaken us for the enemy. I could see the
shells coming, and every time they would fire, I would
fall on my stomach, and thought they all went just
over my head. I was soon, however, out of range,
and began to feel easy, when a new fear took possession of me. What if I had, in my bewilderment,
run into the rebel lines? i saw just ahead of me an
old-fashioned southern mansion, with a high board
fence all around it, and in the inclosure several small
cabins used for the slaves to live in. I could not
remember seeing this before, so I made up my mind
I was actually inside rebeldom. However, I decided
to make the best of it, and if I were or were not I
would see if I could find something to eat. With
fear and faltering steps I moved toward the big gate,
swung it open, and it gave an awful squeak as it
swung on its old rusty hinges. There was not a sign
of life in or about the place, and that gave me hope
and courage. In the center of the yard was a large
hen-house. Cautiously toward this I crawled, heard
the cackle of fowl, went first on one side then on the
other, looking for the door; and imagine my surprise,
the fear that took possession of me—my hair stood
on end ; for sitting there on a bench back of this hen-
house were two big Johnnies. I could'nt speak, I
couldn't move, till one of them said, ''Good evening,

sar ; got anything to eat?" "Yes, yes," I stam-
mered, "I have some hard-tack." Finally, one of
them seeing I was most scared to death, spoke up
and said, "Don't be alarmed ; we are only deserters
and want to give ourselves up ; show us to headquarters." I was brave now. I gave them what
hard-tack I had, and marched them ahead of me back
to the rear, till we found headquarters. Afterward,
I was offered a furlough for capturing two of the
enemy. I never told this before ; I took the credit.
But I was not satisfied; I'd rather have some of those
chickens than live rebels. So back I went and I got
five ; started back to the rear, put a kettle on a
fire and boiled them, kept them three days, till I
found my brother and the remnant of the regiment.
When I did find them I made their hearts glad by
showing them the boiled chickens. They were awful
hungry and set to eating with a ravenous appetite,
but they could not eat them, hungry as they were.
I had no salt, and so put a big chunk of salt beef in
the pot instead of salt, consequently the chickens
were saltier then Lot's wife

I think I felt more disappointed than anybody, so
I determined to make up for it in some other way.
The regiment finally brought up in the first or advance
line of breastwork, and I was still skirmishing in the
rear for anything that I could find that was good.

I had tramped back to the rear about three miles,
my mind bent on securing anything that would please
the heart and eye, or tickle the palates of the brave

fellows who had gone to face the enemy and do the
real work of our country.   About a quarter of a mile
to the left of me I espied a covered wagon moving
toward the front.   I wondered what it was and where
it was bound for, as from the frequent halt it made, it
seemed the driver was lost to himself.   I bore down
toward him and found it was a sanitary wagon, loaded
with good things sent out by the ladies of the north.
The driver was an old man—one of those long, lanky
individuals who might be taken for a parson or a horse
dealer.   He reminded me of the "Arkansaw Traveler."   His clothes were of the salt and pepper home-
spun goods, a little worse for wear and very ill fitting,
they looked as if he had lost fifty pounds of flesh
since he started from home ; his pants were tucked
into a pair of old cow-hide boots ; his hat was a cross
between a stove pipe and a derby ; his hair was red,
very long and sprinkled with grey ; his eyebrows
were shaggy, nearly meeting over the nose and hanging down over a pair of faded blue eyes.   So wrinkled
was his skin that you would think his face was a
frozen laugh ; a little strip of red hair ran down the
side of his face in front of his ears and almost met
under his chin ; the space left open in his whiskers,
evidently an outlet for the tobacco juice that trickled
down from each side of his mouth.   As I approached
he pulled up his mules and called to me in a rather
cracked voice, "Say, Major, or Sergeant, or what
ever you are, whar's the field hospital?"

"Three miles from here," said I, pointing back-
ward.

"What's that firin I hear?   Ain't no rebs 'round yere, be thar?"

"Yes," I replied; "there's a long row of them about half a mile in front of us, and you had better halt right where you are.   What's your cargo?"

"Wall, I got most anything that is needed by you poor fellows—useful things.   I'm sent here by a society called the Northfield First Methodist Ladies' Relief and Sanitary Association.   They selected me for my courage to go to the front and distribute this load.   But I guess I'll have to go too near that row of rebs if I'd give them out in person. I'll unhitch here and feed my mules.   You don't think thar's any danger of them grey-coats disturbing me, do you?   I should hate to have all these good things fall into their hands."

I inquired what he had, to which he replied with apparent amazement : "Shirts, stockins, bakin' powder, condensed milk, canned apples, peaches, Boston beans, tobacco, hair oil, tooth powder, cathartic pills, Jamaiki ginger, and fine tooth combs—— Whoa thar — stop your infernal kickin.   Them durned mules are worse than two-year-old heifers."

The wearied animals had become all tangled up in the harness, and I thought I'd steal some of the eatables for my company while he was freeing and feeding the mules.   He gave me a better opportunity however.   There was a patch of peanuts or ground-nuts a short distance away.   He asked me to mind his mules while he went to see what they were and how **they** grew.   When he left me I got into the

wagon and loaded myself down with everything until
I could carry no more. Then I conceived an
idea, and if he would only remain away long enough
I could carry the thing out. I found a small hatchet
in the wagon, and with my tin cup began digging a
hole near the wagon. I worked like a beaver for
awhile, at the same time keeping my eye on the pea-
nut patch. The size of the receptacle would be determined by the length of time the old man remained
away. Finally I got a hole made about the size of a
bushel basket, and thought I'd take no more chances.
I scrambled into the wagon and threw out cans of
milk, etc., until the hole was completely filled. I
had just nicely covered it up when my friend returned
and asked:

"What you been diggin' for thar—them durned
things too? Why, durn them, I'd just as lieve eat raw
beans."

I looked up in a guilty sort of way and told him,
"I was digging for a shell that lit there while he was
gone."

"Ge-whiz! I guess I'd better get out of this
place as quick as I can. I say, Mister, whar's your
Comp'ny?"

"What's alive of them are at the front, suffering
from want and hunger," I replied in a strong manner,
thinking perhaps he would drive nearer and distribute
his load. But he was bent on going back. As he
climbed to his seat he said, "I'll tell you, Mr. Sergeant, you kin take a few of these things to the men
that are sick in your company."

"They are all sick," I said quickly, for I was greedy and wanted all I could get. He pulled out a hospital shirt and tied up the neck. Having filled it with condensed milk, tobacco, and other things, he asked me if I could carry it. "Could I! I could carry all there's in your cart," I replied. I found my load was a little heavier than I had expected it to be, but I wouldn't say there was too much, but helped him to hitch up his mules and he started off, after giving me a warm hand-shake. I watched him until he disappeared from view, and then thought I would open up the treasure I had buried and deposit some of the shirtful which he had so kindly given me after I had robbed him. It would lighten the load and I could return for the balance next day. I had just started to dig, when I looked up and saw him driving back as hard as he could drive, "Say, young fellow, I—I—I," in a wild, excited manner, reigning his mules up with a jerk and a "Whoa, thar," loud enough to be heard in Petersburg, "I—I thought I'd drive back and dig up that darned shell. It'll be a great curiosity. When I get home I can show the folks the dangerous position I was placed in while distributing these things."

I didn't stop to hear any more, but hurried away with my shirtful. I ran hard and fast, and didn't dare to turn and look round. The shells began to whiz pretty thickly just at this time, and I prayed and hoped that the old man would get scared and not dig for that shell, for I wanted the boys to have it.

This was on the day fixed for the great mine explosion, every soldier on the entire line was waiting with

The Great Mine Explosion in Front of Petersburg.

bated breath for the signal or prolonged rumble of that expected explosion. It did not come, however. The suspense was broken by the appearance nearly a half

a mile away, of a soldier with something white on
his back, that made a good target for the rebel
sharpshooters. Down the railroad I came. I reached
the first line of earthworks. For a short distance I
would keep on top. In this way I kept on, on, first
running one breastwork then another, till I reached
the front line. On top of this I ran the whole length,
heedless and unmindful of the rebel bullets that
pelted about me. I almost flew along. The soldiers
shouted to me to keep down, but I heeded them not.
Finally I reached the place where my regiment was,
jumped down as coolly as if I had run no risk, depos-
ited my bag, received the congratulations of my company, who examined me all over to see if there were
any wounds. They found none, however, but on
opening the shirt every can of milk had a bullet hole
through it, and condensed milk, extract of beef, and
tobacco had to be eaten as a soufflee.

The next day found me at the rear again. I
looked for the buried treasure—found it. Evidently
the old gent had been frightened away, for about half
the dirt had been removed from the top, and the stuff
was not uncovered. There was a desperate fight
going on at the right of our line. I was pressed into
the service of the stretcher corps, which is usually
composed of drummer boys. I did duty at this all
the forenoon. The onslaught was terrible, and many
poor fellows did I help carry off that field ; some to
live for an hour, others to lose a limb that would
prove their valor and courage for the balance of
their lives.

This day our regiment was relieved from the front and supposing they were going to City Point to recruit, they came back about a half a mile, halted for orders; I heard of it and concluded I would go with them and so hastened to where they were, and soon after my arrival the order came to "fall in." They did so with a lacrity and bright hopes of much needed rest. I took my drum and place at the head of the regiment and started with them.

The road to the left led to City Point. Imagine their surprise when nearing it, the order came, " FILE RIGHT, BY COMPANY INTO LINE, DOUBLE QUICK MARCH."

The entire regiment seemed paralyzed for a moment, but only for a moment, the whizzing of the shells and the zip zip of the rebel bullets plainly told them what caused the sudden change. I was dumbfounded, I didn't know what to do. My brother yelled to me to go to the rear quick, but I didn't ; I kept on with them until it seemed to rain bullets, but on, on they went unmindful of the awful storm of leaden messengers of death—on, on and into one of the fiercest charges of the entire war. I saw men fall so thick and fast that there didn't seem as if there was any of my regiment left, and I made up my mind it was too hot for me, so started on the dead run to the rear for a place of safety, and I didn't stop until I was pretty sure I was out of harm's way.

I came to a place about one mile back where evidently there had been a battery located ; here I sat down to rest and meditate. I examined myself all over to see if I was hit, found I was unhurt but my drum had received several bullet holes in it.

Finding a green spot I stretched myself out and listened to the awful sound of musketry firing which was going on at the front, around me on all sides was the debris of a deserted camp, empty tin cans, broken bayonets, pieces of guns, fragments of bursted shell, and occasionally a whole one that had failed to explode. I had only sat here a few moments thinking which was the best way to go when I was joined by another Drummer Boy from a Pennsylvania regiment. We sat down and talked over our exploits, and I thought he was the most profane lad I had ever met. Most every other word he uttered was an oath.

I asked him if he wasn't afraid to talk so.

"What the h—l should I be afraid of?" he asked, at the same time picking up an old tent stake and sticking it into the ground, trying to drive it in with the heel of his boot. Failing in this he reached over and got hold of an unexploded shell and used this on the stake, but it was heavy and unwieldy.

"I wonder if this was fired by those d—d rebs," he asked.

"I guess it was," I replied, "and you better look out, or it might go off."

"Off be d—d, their shells were never worth the powder to blow 'em to h—l, see the hole in the butt of it, it would make a G—d—d good mawl, wouldn't it?" and looking round at the same time he found an old

broom. Stripping the brush and wire from the handle
he said, "I'll make a mawl of it and drive that d—d
rebel stake into the ground with one of their own
d—d shells, be d—d if I don't. Inserting the broom
handle into the end of the shell he walked over to a
stump, and taking the shell in both hands commenced
pounding onto the stick against the stump ; "d—d
tight fit," he hollored to me, and the next instant I
was knocked down by a terrific explosion. I came to
my senses in a minute and hastened to where he had
been standing. There the poor fellow lay uncon-
scious and completely covered with blood, there was
hardly a shred of clothes on him, his hair was all
burned and both hands taken completely off, as if
done by a surgeon's saw.

I was excited and horror stricken for a moment.
The sight was horrible, but I quickly regained my
composure, knowing that something must be done,
and done quickly. So taking the snares from my
drum I wound them tightly around his wrists to stop
the flow of blood, then I hailed an ambulance, and
we took him to the field hospital about a mile to
the rear.

On the way the poor fellow regained conscious-
ness, and looking at his mutilated wrists, and then
with a quick and bewildered glance at me, "G—d—d
tough, ain't it," then the tears started in his eyes, and
he broke down and sobbed the rest of the way, "Oh,
my God! What will my poor mother say? Oh, what
will she do!"

We reached the field hospital, which is only a temporary place for the wounded where the wounds are hurriedly dressed, and then they are sent to regular hospitals, located in Baltimore, Philadelphia, Norfolk, Portsmouth, etc., where they have all the comforts possible.

We laid the little fellow down in one corner of the tent to wait his turn with the surgeon, and when I left him, he cried and begged for me to stay, but I couldn't stand his suffering longer, so I bade him good-bye with tears streaming down my own cheeks. I hurried out, and even after I reached the outside I could hear him cry, "Oh, my God! What will my poor mother say? Oh, what will she do!"

In the afternoon I was detailed to wait on the amputating tables at the field hospital.

It was a horrible task at first. My duty was to hold the sponge or "cone" of ether to the face of the soldier who was to be operated on, and to stand there and see the surgeons cut and saw legs and arms as if they were cutting up swine or sheep, was an ordeal I never wish to go through again. At intervals, when the pile became large, I was obliged to take a load of legs or arms and place them in a trench near by for burial. I could only stand this one day, and after that I shirked all guard duty. The monotony, the routine of life, in front of Petersburg, was becoming distasteful to me. I had stolen everything I could. My district or territory had given out, so the next day I started for the front to bid my brother good-bye.

Our regiment was sometimes relieved and ordered to the rear for rest; so it was on this occasion, they had fallen back and halted in a little ravine. I met my brother, who always expected me to bring him some stolen sweets or goodies of some kind, but unfortunately this time I came empty-handed. I had failed to find anything to steal. I was hungry myself, but when I looked at him I forgot my own hunger, for such a forlorn appearance as he presented almost broke my heart, and I determined to find him something to eat at all hazards. So off I started on an independent foraging expedition. I had only gone a short distance when I espied a "pie wagon." Usually when the paymaster was around there would be "hucksters" or peddlers with all kinds of commodities following in his wake. This fellow had driven to the front from City Point. They were generally dare-devils, and this one was no exception to the rule. He had driven right up to the front, unhitched his horse and began selling hot mince pies. He had some kind of a stove and outfit in an old covered wagon where he made the pies quickly and sold them hot for one dollar apiece; the pies were about the size of a saucer. When I reached the wagon there was quite a crowd around him; some were buying and eating them as if they were good, while others stood looking on wistfully watching their comrades who were fortunate enough to have the price. I was one of the unfortunates. I could smell the cooking of the pies long before I reached the wagon, and this only served to increase my already ravenous hunger;

but all I could do was to stand there with my hands
in my pockets, smack my lips and imagine what they
tasted like—the longer I staid the better they tasted.
I believe I would have given five hundred dollars for
one if I had possessed the money, but I didn't have a
cent; our regiment had not been paid. All this time
I was thinking of my poor brother, how he would like
one of those hot pies, and I began to concoct schemes
how to get one. The way I worked the old sanitary
man would never do to try on this fellow, for he was

a "fakir" by birth, occupation and inclination. The
fellow was doing a lively business. "Here you are!
Nice hot pies, fresh baked, right from the oven!
Walk up lively here. Only one dollar apiece! There's
only a few of them left, and I shan't be here again for
a month; walk up with your dollar! Get off that
wheel, you young devil!" I had climbed up on the
wheel to make observations and see if I couldn't sneak
a pie, but he was watching and detected my motive;
so down I got and stood gaping at him, my mouth

wide open; but my hungry look had no effect on him,
he had no sympathy for anything except dollars.
Finally I thought my brother might have a dollar, so
back to him I ran, told him of the pies, but he had
not a cent. The knowledge of the pies added two
fold to his hunger. "Gosh!" he said, "ain't there
some way? Can't you steal one?" "No," I said, "I
have tried that. I would have made his horse run
away and upset his wagon, but the darned cuss had
unhitched him."

"Ge!" I exclaimed, "I have it." And off I
started. Charley, my brother, owned an old-fashioned
silver watch, one of those old "English levers." He
thought a great deal of it as a keep-sake and always
gave it to me to keep when he was going into action.
I had this watch now, and made up my mind I would
trade it to the "fakir" and get a lot of pies for us all.
Oh! such bright anticipations of hot mince pies. I
could almost see them floating in the air as big as cart
wheels, and fearing they would all be sold before I
could reach the wagon, I ran as hard as I could. The
crowd had thinned out and so had the pies. "How
many have you got left?" I eagerly asked "Oh,
plenty," he replied; "how many do you want?"
"Well," I said, nearly ort of breath, "I haven't any
money, but I want all you have, and I'll trade you
a nice watch for them."

"Say, cully! what yer givin' me? I don't want
no watch. Let's see it."

I quickly passed it up to him, and stood working my fingers and feet impatiently and revolving in

my mind how many pies he would give me and how
I would manage to carry them back, when he broke
out into a loud, contemptuous laugh, and passed the
watch back.

"Say, young fellow, that aint no good. I'd
rather have a blacking box than that thing."

"It's silver," I replied.

"That don't make no difference. I'll give you
one pie for the thing if you want it, see!"

I turned the watch over and over in my hand,
my feelings hurt and my stomach disappointed. Then
I thought of my brother, forgot that it was his high-
priced time-piece, and quickly said:

"Give me the pie and take the watch."

He did so, and away I started on the dead run,
I could hardly resist the temptation of biting the pie;
but just before I reached the regiment, and in full
sight of my brother, I stumbled and fell, smashing the
pie into the dirt and mud. I picked myself up, looked
at the crushed pie, and the tears started in my eyes;
but only for a moment. I brushed them away, gathered
up the pieces and hurried to my brother. We rubbed
the mud from the pieces the best we could, and devoured
them with a hearty relish. After the pie was gone, I regretted the bargain that I had made. Pie and watch
both gone. Remorse took possession of me. I felt
guilty; I was conscience-stricken. I was unsatisfied;
no more time, no more pie.

"Gosh, that pie was good, wasn't it, 'Pod'?"
This was a nickname my brother was pleased to call
me by.

"Jinks, I wish you had brought more. Why didn't you try and get two?"

"Well," I said, faltering, "you—you see, I—I didn't have time enough."

"Well, how did you get it, anyway?"

"Oh! I got it on tick." And then I walked over to a stump, thinking I would get away from his questions and all the time revolving in my mind whether I should tell him the truth, or say I had lost it. I felt ashamed of myself and thought what a darned fool I was. I concluded I wasn't a bit smart—the idea of giving a watch for a pie! Finally, Charley came over to me.

"What time is it, Pod?"

"I—I don't know!"

"Why, ain't the the watch going?"

"Yes-s. No, it's gone."

"Gone! What do you mean?" And then divining the truth, he exclaimed: "Gor-ram it, did you sell the watch for that pie?"

"Yes, Charley, I did, but I couldn't help it; I knew you wanted the pie so bad."

"Gor-rammed little fool; didn't you know better than that?"

Then I saw the great big tears come into his eyes, and I couldn't stand it. I patted him on the back and said: "Never mind, Charley. I'll go and get the watch back if I have to kill the pie man." So off I started on the dead run, caught the fellow just as he was ready to go. I asked him if I could ride to the rear with him. He answered, "Yes, and you can show me how to get into that turnip watch." So I climbed on to the seat beside him and we started. I took the watch apart, showed him how it was wound, set and regulated it, and was about to hand it back to him, when a shell burst a short way from us, which frightened his horse so that he cramped the wagon and upset it, and in the confusion I got lost with the watch. On the next day I gave it to my brother and told him how I had obtained it. He laughed at me, and said he "guess I'd better keep it myself," and so put it in his pocket. That night the regiment went into action, and my brother was slightly wounded several times. One shot would have proved fatal, but the watch received the bullet and the wound proved fatal only to the watch; it was smashed all to pieces. But my brother prizes the pieces now more than he ever did the whole watch.

The next day my regiment was ordered to the front again. I made up my mind I would not go with them. I concluded I needed rest in order to recuperate, so when the regiment started I bade my brother good-bye, gave him a parting kiss and God's blessings, so off I started.

About a half a mile from my regiment I came to one of those Virginia fences, got up on top of it, and sat thinking, and while sitting there the shells began to fly pretty thick. I thought I had better be moving, jumped down, and as I did so a shell struck one of the rails of the fence. A piece of the rail struck me and was harder than I was, for when I came to my senses I found I was in the hospital. I didn't think I was hurt very badly, but when I tried to get up, found I couldn't. From there they moved me to "Balfour Hospital" at Portsmouth, Virginia. I never will forget the shame and mortification I felt at the sight I must have presented when the boat that conveyed us to Portsmouth arrived.

An old negro came to my bunk and took me on his back, and with a boot in each hand dangling over his shoulder he carried me pickaback through the streets to the hospital, a large, fine building, formerly the "Balfour Hotel," and converted into a hospital after Portsmouth was captured. They took me up stairs into what was formerly the dining-room but now filled with over two hundred little iron beds, and each bed occupied by a wounded soldier. Everything in and about the place was as neat as wax. They carried me to a vacant bed near the center of the room, and I noticed the next bed to mine had several tin dishes hanging over it, suspended from the ceiling. These were filled with water, and from a small hole punctured in the bottom the water would slowly but constantly drip upon some poor fellow's wound to keep it moist. I had just sat down on the side of my bed, when I was startled by the sound of a familiar voice. "Hello, cully! What you been doin', playing with one of those d—d shells, too?"

No, I replied, the shells were playing with me. Then I recognized the occupant of the next bed as my drummer boy acquaintance who had his hands blown off a week ago. What a strange thing that we should be brought together side by side again, both wounded with a shell and nearly on the same spot.

He had changed wonderfully; his little white pinched face told too plainly the suffering he had endured. I asked him how he was getting along.

"Oh I'm getting along pretty d—d fast. I guess I'll croak in a few days.'

"Oh you musn't talk that way, you'll be all right in a little while."

Oh, no, cully, I know better. I'm a goner; I know it. I don't want to live, anyhow. What in h—l is the good of a man without hands?" Then turning his bandaged head towards me, his eyes filling with tears. "I aint afraid to die, cul., but I would like to see my old mother first. Do you think I will?"

Oh, yes, I said, no doubt of it; at the same time I felt that his days were numbered, but I wanted to make him feel as comfortable as possible. He was so much worse off than I, that I forgot my own injuries and was eager to assist him all I could. After a few minutes silence—

"Say, cully, reach under my pillow and find a little book there; it's a little Testament that my dear old mother gave me; read a little for me, will you please? You'll find a place mother marked for me, read that, please."

I turned the leaves over till I found a little white ribbon pinned to a leaf, marking the verse beginning, "Suffer little children to come unto me." I started to read for him, but the tears filled my eyes. I had to stop, and as I did so, I noticed he seemed very quiet. I glanced at him, and the open, staring eyes and the rigid drawn features told me too plainly that . the little fellow was out of his sufferings:—he was dead!

"Mother" was the countersign on his lips so thin,
And the sentry in heaven *must* let him in.

I remained here three weeks, finally got up and around and began to think I had enough of soldier life. I had everything I wished for ; some ladies in the town—God bless them, I never will forget them— visited the hospital occasionally, and they always took pains to bring me flowers or goodies of some kind. (Pardon me, but somehow I was always a favorite with ladies.) Well, after remaining there three or four weeks I concluded I didn't want to go to the front, so I sat down and wrote a personal letter to Secretary Stanton, told him who, how, and what I was, and asked him to advise me what to do ; if I should go to the front or home. Soon after, a special order came back from him to have me transferred to the " 2nd Battalion Veteran Reserve Corps."

Let me here state to those who do not under- stand ; all soldiers who were sick or wounded, unfit for field service were transferred to the Veteran Reserve Corps, for the purpose of doing light guard duty in camp, or at headquarters ; they were divided into two battalions, 1st and 2nd. The 1st battalion was supposed to be able to carry a musket for duty, while the 2nd battalion was composed of one-armed men or totally disabled soldiers, and were supplied

with a small sword; and thus I was condemned by
special order; however I liked it.   I had an easy time,
nothing to do, and others to help me.

I continued here for about two months, until the
hospital was ordered to be removed to Old Point
Comfort.   I had become a great favorite of Lieutenant
Russell, the officer in charge of the hospital, and a
nice man he was.   When the order came to move,
the fixtures, furniture, in fact everything in and about
the building was ordered to be sold.   I was detailed
by Lieutenant Russell to remain behind and superin-
tend the sale of the stuff, keep accounts, make a report when all was sold, and turn over the proceeds.
That detained me there two weeks longer.   I sold the
beds, dishes, tables, everything.   There remained
about thirty tons of coal in the yard to be disposed
of.   I sold it in any quantity to poor people; took any
price for it I could get, the same as everything else.
Finally, everything was sold off, and I was ready to
depart the next day for Old Point Comfort.   In the
evening, the two men I had with me and myself, used to
get our pipes and sit in front of the office and smoke.
We were sitting there talking about the sale, when it
occurred to me that I had overlooked the "dead-
house."   We went back to it and found seven coffins.
What was to be done ; they must be sold, as they
must be accounted for, and we were going to depart
early in the morning.   The street was crowded at
that time in the evening, so I took the coffins and
stood them up on the sidewalk, and everyone that
passed by, I would ask him if he wanted to buy a

coffin. Finally, I struck a man who offered me seven dollars for the lot, and I took it quick. I learned afterward he was an undertaker.

The next day I landed and reported to head-quarters at Fortress Monroe. A day or two after, Lieutenant Russell sent for me; he wanted a foreman in the Government Printing Office. I was down for occupation on the pay-roll as a printer. He asked me if I understood the business. I said yes, I had some knowledge of it, so I was detailed with an extra eight dollars per month. I took charge of the office at once. The first day I had orders to print fifty thousand official envelopes. The press-boy brought me the proof, I looked it over, and marked it correct; they were printed and sent to headquarters.

A few days after Lieutenant Russell sent for me to report at his office. I didn't know what was up. Thought perhaps I was going to be sent to Washington to take charge of the Government Printing Office there. As I went in, the lieutenant turned to me with a quizzical smile on his face:

"Young man, you told me you were a printer?"

"Yes, sir."

"Did you 'O. K.' this job?" passing one of the envelopes he held in his hand.

"Yes sir," I answered.

"Umph! Is it correct?"

"Yes, sir."

"It is, eh?"

"Yes-s, sir."

"Umph! how do you spell business?"

Fortress Monroe where Jefferson Davis was Incarcerated.

" B-u-i-s-n-e-ss," said I.

" You do, eh ?"

" Yes, sir."

" Well," said he in an imperative manner, "our government sees fit to differ with you. You will go to your office and print fifty thousand more, but see that you spell business right, and bring me the proof. The lot you have printed we will send to Washington, and recommend that they be made into a paper mache statue of yourself, and label it 'Buisness' or the only government printer."

I was a little chagrined at the mistake, but did not take it to heart; but I was soon relieved by a man who was more careful in his spelling. A week or so after leaving the printing office, I was sent to the fort to act as a kind of a companion to the confederate president, Jefferson Davis. I was instructed to walk and talk with him. I presume I was intended for a sort of guard. Perhaps our government wished to make him feel as if he were not under surveillance, and so placed one whose insignificant appearance would put him at his ease. However, I found it a very agreeable occupation. One of the most pleasant weeks I ever passed was with Mr. Jefferson Davis. He was a most agreeable man to me. He gave me lots of good advice, and I learned more from conversation with him about national affairs than I ever expected to know; and if I ever become president I will avail myself of the advice and teaching of that great man. He pointed out the right and wrong paths for young men ; urged me above all things to adhere

strictly to honesty and integrity ; to follow these two
principles, and I would succeed in business and
become great and respected.   I thanked him for
his kind advice, and pressed his hand good-bye.
"Good-bye, my boy," said he.   "You have been a
comfort to me in my loneliness and sorrow.   God
bless you, my boy, God bless you !"   A great, big
something came up in my throat as I turned and left
him, and I have regretted all my life that I was not
fortunate enough to have the pleasure of meeting him
again before he passed away ; for I assure you, in-
dulgent readers and comrades, that no matter what
he had done, or what mistakes he had made, his
memory will always find a warm spot in the heart of
that little Drummer Boy from Maine.

One day, soon after this I sauntered down to
the steamboat landing and was leisurly beguiling
my time with a very large cigar.   I noticed some
comotion in the harbor but paid more attention to the
cigar than anything else.   Finally a large ocean
steamer came in sight, rounded up near the wharf
and let go her anchor.   Very soon a "cutter" was
lowered manned with sailors and pulled with steady
stroke toward the wharf.   While watching and
wondering what they were going to do with the
soldiers which I saw the vessel was loaded with,
the "gig" or "cutter" neared the wharf, then I
noticed particularly the young officer who sat in the
stern, he was very dictatorial and pompous in his
orders to the sailors, so much so that I said to myself,

that fellow is putting on lots of airs ; he thinks he's some pumpkins, I wish he'd fall overboard.

They finally reached the foot of the stairs, which led to the wharf. The young officer espied me and standing up in the boat shading his eyes with his hand seemed carefully contemplating me. I wondered if it could be possible that he had defined my wish and would have me arrested when he landed ; perhaps it was the cigar that attracted his attention. It was against orders to smoke on the wharf, and such a big cigar in a boy's mouth looked very much out of place, but I wasn't going to give it up, and puffed more vigorously than ever. Just then the "cutter" touched the stairs that led up to the wharf with a bump, and the young officer with his handsome uniform turned a back-summersault overboard. It tickled me to death; I sat down and laughed to see him floundering to reach the stairs. I clapped my hands and cried, "Good, good!" He finally reached the stairs, clambered up onto them, but they being very slippery from the slime left by the ebbing tide, he lost his footing, his heels went into the air, and down again headfirst he went into the ocean. I think he went clear to the bottom, for when he came up he was covered over with sea grass and mud. I laughed harder than before ; everybody laughed, even the sailors, they couldn't help it, and when they fished him out he was a sight! The starch was out of his clothes, but not his pomposity. He roundly blamed the poor sailors. I sang out: "It wasn't their fault; what are you blaming them for?" He looked at me and shook his first. "Well, it wasn't!" and I thought to myself if I were they I would push him in again. I then made up my mind I had better run, but I was so convulsed with laughter that I couldn't move. Huriedly but cautiously climbing the slippery stairs, he made his way straight for me. I was still laughing, so hearty that my eyes were dimmed with tears! but I still puffed away at the big cigar. He looked at me for a moment, then hitting the cigar knocked it overboard, at the same time exclaiming, "You're too young to smoke. What you laughing at? Why don't you salute me? Discipline! I'll teach you discipline, confound you," at the same time boxing my ears. "You "gorramed" little cuss, why don't you salute me?" At the word "Gorrame" I recovered myself, looked up and recognized my brother; he had been promoted since I saw him, had raised a full beard and was in command of a regiment on his way to New Orleans and had run into Fortress Monroe for orders and hoping to find me. I was more than pleased to see him, but wouldn't salute him untill he had soundly cuffed my ears and threatened to throw me into the water.

When he was ready to depart he gave me a cigar and told me I could smoke it after he had gone, but I didn't; just as he was getting into the "cutter," I gave it to the Boatswain. I don't know, but I believe that cigar was loaded.

Soon after this episode, peace was declared, and the orders came to discharge all soldiers and send them to their respective homes, and on the 30th day

VOLUNTEER DESCRIPTIVE LIST and ... ... of Private ... Company of

NOTES

REMARKS

Station
Date

I certify that the above is a ... from the Records of

... during the C company

of June, 1865, the boy who had worked so hard to
get mustered into the service of Uncle Sam was dis-
charged and mustered out. Then I went home to my
dear, anxious family. I was not all covered with glory
and I did not feel that I had saved my country, but was
satisfied that I had not killed anyone ; satisfied that I
had furnished some little comfort and good cheer to
my comrades during their hardships, and above all
that I had learned the glorious distinction of being
entitled to wear one of those little bronze buttons made
from captured cannons and symbolic of the G. A. R.

Having spoken so often of my brother, some one
may ask and wonder what became of him,

During the war our soldiers would often receive
little useful articles, such as stockings, shirts, etc.,
made by the ladies who formed themselves into
societies all over the country and furnished these
things for distribution among the soldiers at the front.
The young ladies had a great craze at that time of
marking their names or initials upon whatever
they made. One day my brother received a pair
of hand-knit stockings with a little tag sewed on each
of them, and written on the tags the letters L. A.
D., Islesboro, Maine. They were so acceptable at the
time that he declared that if he lived to get out of
the army, he would be "gorramed" if he didn't find
the girl that built those stockings, and kiss her for them.
He began writing to Islesboro, making inquiries,
and received several letters signed "Tab." He
was determined not to give it up, however, and
when mustered out, the first thing he did, was

to go to Islesboro, Maine, to find "Tab." He found her, she was a schoolma'm, and soon after married her, and they are now living way out in Port Angeles in the State of Washington happy as bugs in a rug, and every meal time you can find several little "Tabs" around the table, some large enough to tell the story of how Pa found Ma, and a great desire to try the same thing themselves.

The unhappy war was over. The soldier boy returned. I arrived home at the little farm, found a royal, loving welcome from my father and brothers, and more than any other, my little step-sister, who never got tired of stories of my experience. She would sit for hours, begging me to tell her more. She was always with me wherever I would go. She was full of admiration for me. I was a hero in her eyes ; I could not dispel her fancy, and I didn't try, for she seemed the sunshine of my life. She plodded with me through all my ups and downs ; through the snow and ice of winter, making summer for me the year round, and she is now my little wife.

I must stop here, or I may go too far into a history of my life, which I did not intend. I know it would be uninteresting, but will simply add that myself and wife adopted the stage as a profession, and still follow it. I have just completed a play entitled, "The Volunteer" which I shall soon submit for public approval.

My recollections are finished—for they are but recollections of a time that "tried men's souls." In looking back o'er the path of life there is a melancholy pleasure, to me, at least, in contemplating the shattered shards of many an air built castle,—inhaling the perfumes of flowers long since faded and dead. If these reflections have served to beguile one moment of "ennui" for an idle reader—if they have recalled ONE incident of "derring doe" to a whilesome comrade, I am satisfied that my purpose is accomplished.

CACTUS CREAM ✳ ✳

The Most Elegant and Delicate Preparation

✳ ## FOR THE SKIN

EVER DISCOVERED.

IT POSITIVELY REMOVES :
{ FRECKLES,
BLACKHEADS,
PIMPLES,
MORPHEW,
TAN,

And all Blemishes of Cuticle.

—→>◇<←—

- - CACTUS CREAM Is used all over the world in preference to any other preparation for the complexion. A beautiful effect is discernible after the first application, and its continued use only increases the beauty of the skin until an exquisite complexion is obtained.

For Creating, Restoring, Preserving and Insuring Beauty,

Nothing has ever been found one-half so effective and satisfactory as **Cactus Cream.** By its use the roughest skin is made to rival the pure radiant texture of **Youthful Beauty.** **Redness, Pimples** and **Blotches** are quickly overcome by the healing and cooling properties of **Cactus Cream,** and a satin-like smoothness of the skin of great beauty is soon acquired.

Sunburn, **Freckles** and **Tan** removed by faithfully applying **Cactus Cream.**

Applied to the **Neck, Arms** and **Hands,** it gives an appearance of **Graceful Rotundity,** as well as **Pearly Blooming Purity.**

Cactus Cream eradicates everything that mars the beauty of the complexion and adds the tint of the lily. Gentlemen find it cool and refreshing when used after shaving. **All Barbers use it.**

———— • ————

FOR SALE BY DRUGGISTS, HAIR DRESSERS, Etc.,

25 CENTS PER BOTTLE,

Prepaid by Mail to any Address.

——o——

CHILES & CO., SOLE MANUFACTURERS AND PROPRIETORS. CHICAGO.

718 CHAMBER OF COMMERCE.

Read This Carefully.

When you arrive in Chicago, stop at the best hotel in the world, the

"SHERMAN HOUSE"

EVERY ROOM SPACIOUS AND ELEGANTLY FURNISHED!

THE CUSINE IS UNEXCELLED!

Agreeable courteous clerks, attentive waiters, and meals served without spoiling. In fact a hotel you fe l at home in.

RATES: $3.00, $3 50, $4.00, $4.50 and $5.00.

SPECIAL RATES TO THE THEATRICAL PROFESSION.

CENTRAL LOCATION: COR. CLARK AND RANDOLPH STREETS.

J. IRVING PEARCE, PROPRIETOR.

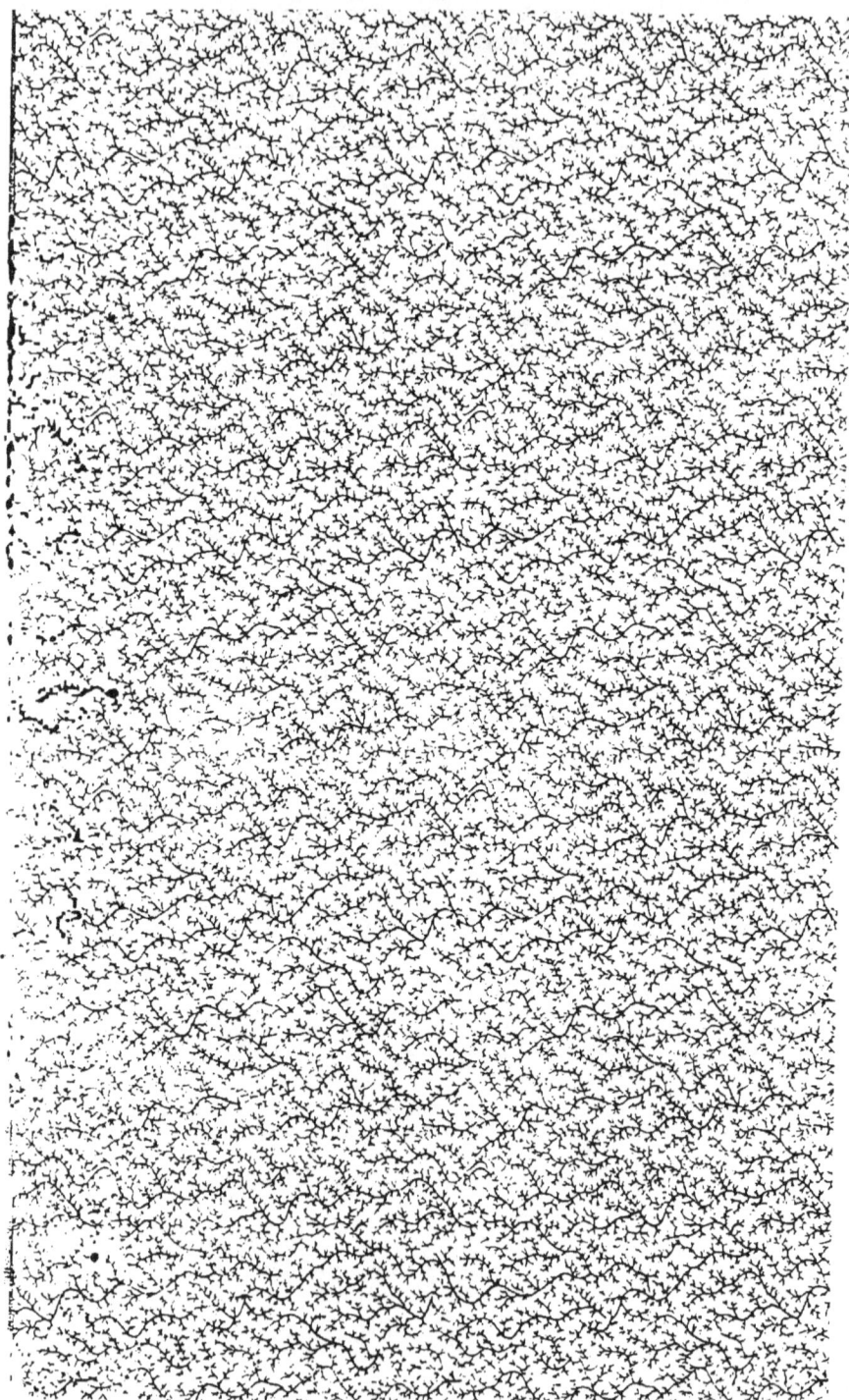

www.ingramcontent.com/pod-product-compliance
Lightning Source LLC
Chambersburg PA
CBHW032242080426
42735CB00008B/966